W9-BSS-148

United States Army

by Julie Murray

ABDO
U.S. ARMED FORCES
Kids

www.abdopublishing.com

Published by Abdo Kids, a division of ABDO, PO Box 398166, Minneapolis, Minnesota 55439.

Printed in the United States of America, North Mankato, Minnesota.

052014

092014

**THIS BOOK CONTAINS
RECYCLED MATERIALS**

Photo Credits: AP Images, Getty Images, iStock, Shutterstock, Thinkstock,
© Keith McIntyre / Shutterstock p.1, © The U.S. Army / CC-BY-2.0 p13,15,21

Production Contributors: Teddy Borth, Jennie Forsberg, Grace Hansen

Design Contributors: Candice Keimig, Laura Rask, Dorothy Toth

Library of Congress Control Number: 2013953954

Cataloging-in-Publication Data

Murray, Julie.

 United States Army / Julie Murray.

   p. cm. -- (U.S. Armed Forces)

ISBN 978-1-62970-094-6 (lib. bdg.)

Includes bibliographical references and index.

1. United States Army--Juvenile literature.   I. Title.

355.00973--dc23

        2013953954

Table of Contents

United States Army

The Army is the largest branch of the U.S. **Armed Forces**. They fight battles on the ground.

The Army's main job

is to keep the U.S. safe.

6

Gear

The Army uses lots of gear.

They use night vision goggles

to see at night.

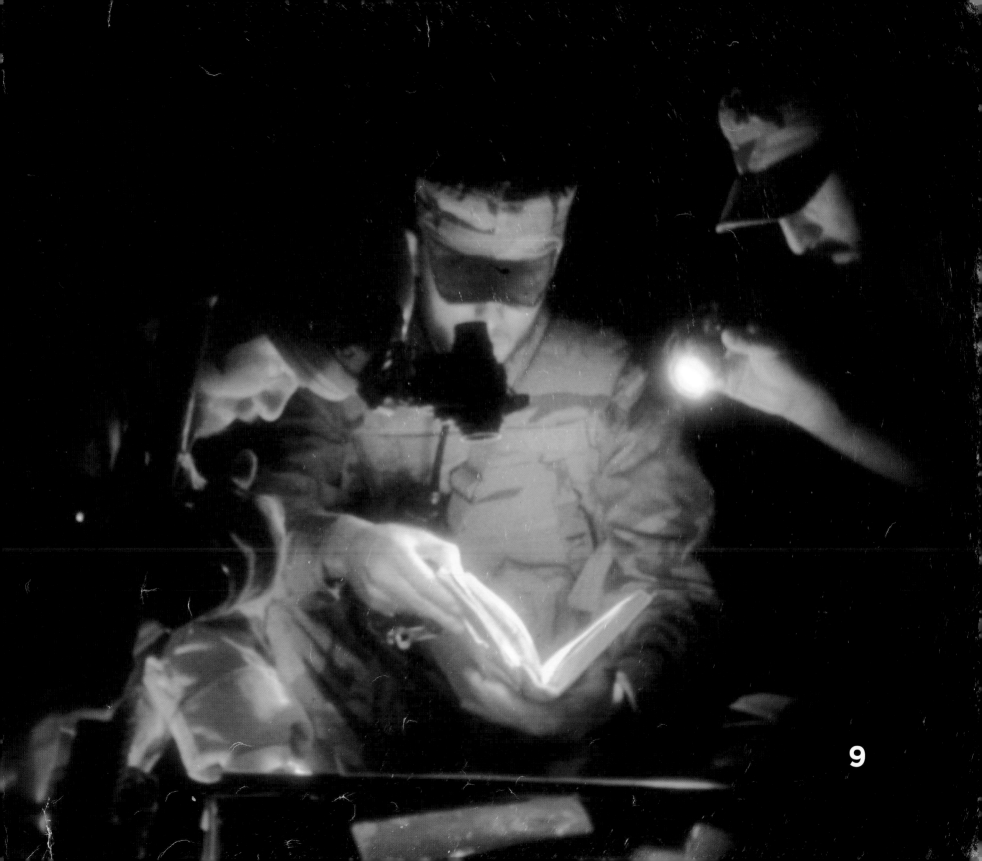

9

They use **camouflage** suits. They also use **GPS** to find locations.

11

Vehicles and Weapons

The Army uses many

different weapons.

They use guns in battles.

They use fighting **vehicles**. The

M2 Bradley is a fighting vehicle.

They also use helicopters. The

AH-64A Apache is a helicopter.

14

Jobs

There are many different

jobs in the Army. **Medics**

give first aid to hurt soldiers.

16

Paratroopers parachute into battle. Cooks prepare meals for soldiers.

19

"This We'll Defend"

The Army keeps Americans

safe every day!

More Facts

- Thirty of the forty-four U.S. presidents served in the Army. Twenty-four of those presidents served during wartime.

- George Washington was not only the first president of the United States. He was also the U.S. Army's first commander.

- The U.S. Army is older than the United States of America. The army was born June 14, 1775. The United States of America was born on July 4, 1776.

Glossary

armed forces – military (land), naval (sea), and air forces (air). They protect and serve their nation.

camouflage – a special pattern and colors on clothing that allows the person wearing it to blend into their surroundings.

GPS – An abbreviation for Global Positioning System. It uses satellites in space to find the position of a vehicle, person, or other objects.

medic – a member of the military medical corps. If a soldier is injured, a medic is there to help.

vehicle – any means by which to travel. A car is a vehicle. Even a sled is a vehicle.

weapon – any object that is used in defense in combat.

Index

abdokids.com

Use this code to log on to abdokids.com and access crafts, games, videos and more!

Abdo Kids Code:
UUK0946